spar

spar Words in Place
Peter Sanger

GASPEREAU PRESS   MMII

For M.

... anyone who rests content merely with the
sign will never get to the interior truth.

In eternity there is only oneness, but not likeness.

MEISTER ECKHART

Table of Contents

Foreword

These essays are pauses during which I looked at the map. Their concerns are the ways in which we take words with us when we journey, what they do with our conversation while we travel and how we may learn to live with their consequence when we have found a destination. The first of the essays was written and published in 1984. The last was completed a few months before this book went to press. All four are offered here in chronological order. Any reader curious about the length of time and the stages it took me to get from one place to the next will find dates and circumstances of publication among the notes at the end. I have revised the original texts of the first three essays to correct mistakes of style, fact, and typography.

Thoreau titled one of his last and finest essays "Walking." That title might have suited this collection. At some point each of its essays involves walking one way or another, although perhaps each is only an excursions in the same direction. But I could not appropriate Thoreau's title and imply close comparisons. At best I trust that this collection, like his essay, speaks a word for Nature and that it does so in the spirit of sauntering, a word which Thoreau, at the beginning of his essay, derives "in the good sense" from a designation for pilgrims "going *à la Sainte Terre*" or for those "*sans terre*" who "are equally at home everywhere."[1] Walter Skeat in his *Etymological Dictionary of the English Language* – published in 1882, twenty years after Thoreau finished "Walking" – called both derivations "puer-ilities."[2] Perhaps he did not know Thoreau's essay, or else he knew it (as he thought) only too well and did not really know it at all. For we can both insist upon etymological pre-cisions and value the accumulation of co-inherent meanings which human imagination and ethical necessities add to them. Thoreau, *sans terre* in the good sense, eventually journeyed with his work *à la sainte terre* where earth is sacred and unap-propriated. His dying words were "moose" and "Indian." For seeing and speaking another such country a poet might hope.

SOUTH MAITLAND
NOVA SCOTIA

14

Biorachan Road

The road is mud and gravel. Depending on where you have been and where you are going, it begins or ends at Highway 311, just outside the village of Earltown, north Colchester County, Nova Scotia. From there it climbs and falls northeasterly over one of the blunt flanks of the Cobequid Mountains to join Highway 356 just above West Branch River John, Pictou County.

Try saying the road's name. It resists English. Remember picking a blueberry, rubbing its nap clear on your sleeve until – the berry shone. Rub a bit more, and you uncover a duplicity: only the road's sign at Earltown reads, "Biorachan." Five miles away, over the mountain and in another county at West Branch River John, the road's sign reads, "Berichon." Somewhere along its unsettled length, the road has slipped almost free of a Gaelic derivation to assume an anglicized phonetic convenience.

The road was named in the 1820s by Scottish settlers evicted during the Highland Clearances in Sutherlandshire. For another fifty years, until monolingual schooling took hold, Gaelic was spoken in Earltown and thereabouts more commonly than English. As in Cape Breton, church services were held in Gaelic. A shorter English service often followed. But now, locally, Gaelic has almost disappeared. I have heard a word or two of it only once in a fragment of inherited song that not even the singer could translate. Only "Biorachan," or "Berichon," remains, and one other place name similarly wrung in English, "Cnac na Spidial," brought intact from Sutherlandshire, made over to Spidell Hill.

No one seems to be quite sure what "Biorachan" means. When people whose Gaelic-speaking ancestors settled Earltown learned that I was helping to organize a Gaelic poetry festival in Cape Breton in the summer of 1978, they made me promise to find out the meaning of "Biorachan" from the Scottish Gaelic poets invited. But not Derick Thomson, nor Iain Crichton Smith, nor Donald MacAulay could tell with certainty. Together, they guessed derivation from "*biorach*" – pointed, sharp – and it is true that, although the mountain is low, the road is narrow and picks through declivities and around hillocks like an agile needle. But MacAlpine and Mackenzie's Gaelic dictionary gives two other possible meanings, both nouns: "heifer" and (from Skye) "colt."

Some philologist might resolve, or at least put into order, this confusion. But the point seems to be that, in the case of the Biorachan Road, the truth is the very absence of neat certainty, the equivocation of it, together with the ways in which that equivocation is discovered. The facts retreat as they are examined behind one cultural overlay after another; and the series of recessions thus created is at least as complex as that by which imagination might transmute them into art or memory. Time itself has worked as an artist, not preserving the word "Biorachan" as it was, but as it has become, partly on the way to incomprehensibility and alive with latencies. Truth involves using the word in ways that confirm, not abuse, or simplify, or deny ambiguities and contradictions.

The word's meaning is defined not only by cultural forces, but also by the natural happenstance that it represents. "Biorachan" is a connection of minute, objective particulars. To understand further the road's name and to understand the particulars, you must walk. During certain times of the year admittedly, there is the alternative of driving. If you do, you may surprise, as I did once, the red-tailed hawk on another road, trailing a freshly-killed rabbit, jesses of stripped flesh and ripped skin suddenly snagging an alder and torn free. Accidents like that have their place; but so also does the tradition of other, slower rhythms by which they are defined. Once, such slower rhythms in poetry accompanied the rhythms of work. This was true in Scotland, where rowing, weaving, spinning, churning, flailing, and scything all had their songs and poems. Now, one of the few such sources left is the one of walking.

I know a poet who was briefly mad. He explained to me how madness suddenly imprisoned him in systems of interlocking archetypes of great dignity, but essential inhumanity. As he recovered, he felt the sanity of small, exact things, of each individual leaf, of each different birdsong, and the possibility of change and free will existing in no really provable way among natural instincts and necessities. He found that unless he allowed them attributes of particular identity, change, and free will, the symbols in his work would become sterile allegories, which only he could explain, and not even he could inhabit. Now he tries to watch the detail of words and things – by stopping, by waiting, by walking. At least what he said made sense enough to persuade me to walk the road again.

There had been a fair snowstorm a few days before, but not enough for snowshoes. I began the road from the Berichon side. On the first valley mile of the road, there are a few houses and two new house-trailers. When I first travelled the road about ten years ago, there were only four nineteenth-century houses – two used by farmers; one semiabandoned;

and the fourth, a farmhouse without a farm. There were no house-trailers. During the last three or four years, one of the old farmhouses has been levelled and replaced by a circular one. There are two other new houses on the lower part of the road, both single-story bungalows. They look stranded, as if a wave had lifted them from their original suburb into a freedom they can never accommodate. A fourth new house has been built at the top of the valley where the Berichon leaves cleared land behind. You have seen such houses and wondered why the intention of creating a home to fit its environment so often builds goggled angularities of peeled wood.

I know some of the people who live on this part of the road, knew them better once than now. They and their houses and house-trailers are part of the same pattern of tenacity and dissolution as the Berichon itself. A few of the people, like those who first built and named the road, are exiles who left societies emptying of moral authority. Without them and those who stayed, the road would decay. Its gravel would spread and choke the ditches. Its camber would flatten, then invert. Its surface would change in season to silt and sluice away. As quickly as a child grows, the right-of-way would thicken with alders, spruce, shadbush, and pin cherry. Even so, and perhaps for more than a millennium, the road would reveal itself from the air as a manipulation on the earth.

There are places during its first mile, though the passage of cars, tractors, road scrapers, and snowplows has rationalized its course into straightness, where the road still shows how it began. It veers right in the slight dips before small hills, which it then climbs cross-face, veering leftward. No man or animal approaches such hills directly by choice. Each ranges right for the sinistral climb as if ground were a fulcrum. Further up, beyond houses, fields, and the valley, the road becomes more obviously part of an older technology, one that climbed obliquely and descended by short steps, wheel drags down and a wagon load threatening the team. It was a time when the simplest examples of inertia, velocity, and gravity were wrought to work in coherence like words in a sentence. Here the snowplow stops, leaving a barrier of slush and gravel across the road. No one has walked beyond it. No one. At least, you can almost believe so.

The first step is like the first mark on a page. A chickadee sings one whispy rasp, staying hidden. The snow is crustless, but resistant. It lets you sink to the level where your weight just starts to turn it solid, then slips down again, a little, as you push from the ball of your foot and toes to take another stride. You walk hobbled until you learn how to flatten your steps and keep their lift low, skimming the fresh, loose skiff.

There are wind sounds around, always elsewhere, over left, over right, ahead, or behind, while the place where you stand to hear them is estranged in silence. The wind sounds are tree sounds. The road defines a kingdom of trees, all second or later growth. Beech trees and maples, unravelling birches, white, black, red spruce, and a few hemlocks growing with their peculiar dignity and generosity. Many of the beeches, especially the smaller ones, still bear a few leaves which have dried the colour of copper. They vibrate against one another: wind rattles. At the tips of their branches are embryonic *fleurs-de-lis* of bud.

The streams which cross under through rotting wooden culverts and the ditches which run beside the road are open. The ditches keep open by some slight weep of current. Inside them, as if under a bell jar, are grey leaves, fragments of leaves, and mosses disintegrating into cloudy suspensions like spawn. If you touch any of these, they feel supple, but the warmth of the water which keeps them so seems colder than the air. If you draw a leaf out and throw it down on the snow, it will freeze crisp in a few minutes. The streams, by contrast, have cleared themselves of last year's leaves in the fall freshets. They now feed out of themselves another impediment: ice. It has formed in caps and capes over every stone whose tip projects slightly above the surface. Water flutters beneath their upstream edges like a bird at a window. It flows with high-pitched sounds that carry weakly. Often you must stand above the stream, where it flows under the road, before you can hear it and know that it issues so closely.

Where the road climbs steeply, it is cut into the mountain as a ledge. On one side are runs of wooded gully. On the other is packed rock: conglomerate, shale, and slate. The working of the earth and the contractions of winter have split the slate into narrow vertical or slightly angled fragments, fitted and balanced together like a drystone wall. Where water has spilled slowly over the rock's less steep surfaces from the forest humus above, it has frozen into a skin of umbered opaqueness or trickled frozen portcullises or icicles across the gape of lateral fissures. All this is as if the mountain has become a metaphor of growth and change, replenishing itself from verifying parallels, seasonal parodies of the forces which originally made it.

For the road and roadside are filled, even in winter, with similitudes and transformations. There are plumes of golden-rod looking brittle and dry, but soft to touch as the bloom on a plum. Everlasting plants are here in clumps, dry, not lasting, blurring in fuzz, mottled like a spring rabbit's fur. There are raspberry sprays, arching in wide curves, studded by tough five-armed stars that once clamped fruit, and by the tight, pointed cowls in which next year's leaves are growing. Coarse but pliant ravels of greyish green lichen hang from tree trunks and branches. Beeches are cataracted with scales of fungi, but give back the winter light as if it emanated from their bark rather than from the sky and snow. Where one spruce tree has been struck and opened by a falling limb, it looks as if a door had been built to enter the heartwood.

After climbing steeply and twisting for nearly a mile out of the valley of farms, houses, and house-trailers on the Berichon side, the road straightens upon the flattening mountain. Midway to the Biorachan side and Earltown it crosses a plateau half-a-mile wide. This is the mountain's diffused summit. When I first travelled the road and for a few years after, I used to pick blueberries here on a wild barren around the only house still standing on the road's upper length. The house was deserted. Its outbuildings had vanished. So also had its window sashes, doors, shelves, cupboards, wainscoting, bannisters, goodly hemlock wall boards, and whatever else could be used for anything but kindling. It was a shell, as complete from a distance but as empty within as the nymphal husk of a mayfly. So light the house felt that you thought it might take to the air like a kite. Only hunters still used it. You could find their spent cartridges and vacant bottles on the floors of the upstairs bedrooms where they watched at daybreak and dusk for crossing deer. But the house has gone. The barren has been tended, burned, its margins squared and shifted out to end in static turbulences of shoved shrubs and trees. Where the house was is a snow-filled cellar space.

Low blueberry bushes grow on the barren in patches. Some show as small, bare, straight twigs jutting above the snow like stripped quills. Other patches are filled with blueberry plants which have held their leaves. Cold has turned them a dark copper colour. They break with a snap, like wing casings on a dead June bug. Seen from only a few yards away, their copper loses its glint and turns dull brown. There is no visible garden here, only a garden of snow. On a blueberry barren, life in winter is almost imperceptible. A slight fold in the snow, like a wind flaw on water, wavers across the old track which served the house. If you handle that flaw, your fingers break a field mouse road, drilled over the mountain, under the snow, from where to whence, by how and why.

It is the Biorachan now which slopes away on one side of the barren to Earltown. Where the road and barren touch at a corner, there is a new sign, printed on cardboard, stapled to a piece of plywood, nailed on a large birch stump: "No Trespassing Poison Berries per Bragg Lumber Co." Are those threats empty or full? Who washes them clean? Is poison part of the price? What dies to save it? Rub out the nap with your sleeve.

I imagine asking the poet who advised me to walk the road to meet me there, at that sign. Given his anxiety for summits and centres and symmetry, no doubt he would insist that he had to walk from the Biorachan side. I can think of him passing the garage and snowplow shed, where the road joins Highway 311, and then climbing by Earltown Cemetery, where the Fergusons, Baillies, Sutherlands, MacKays, Rosses, and Macdonalds who travelled the road before him are buried. Would he notice how many of the gravestones state the name of the Sutherlandshire parish to which the dead belonged, as if Earltown settlement, Nova Scotia, and what was to become Canada were all insubstantially transient? But I cannot will him to see such things. He sees what he tells.

If I were to see him walking up the hill toward the sign, I might wonder from which century he came: the eighteenth, in which the road namers were born; the nineteenth, when they used it; the twentieth, in which I am writing about it; or perhaps the twenty-first, when it will change further. Would he say all four, or try to return such a question to the level it attempted to transcend by lecturing me on the survival of the pentatonic and asking why Traherne left the fifth of his five *Centuries* incomplete? We might talk. He might listen, then leave, when I took the Berichon back.

The Crooked Knife

There are eight knives on the table now. Some were bought, others given. Six are Mi'kmaq, one Cherokee; and the eighth, because of a carving on its haft, must have been made in the Pacific Northwest.

Although invented and still used by North American Indians, crooked knives are also, in part, European. Some writers trace the design to farriers' curl-tipped hoof-trimming knives. Others believe that during early years of European contact, beaver-tooth blades in Indian carving tools – hafted and used the same way as crooked knives – were simply replaced by metal blades, made then, as frequently now, from worn-out metal files. Given many similar situations in the general development of all languages and cultures, there is no reason why either theory of origin contradicts the other. Both may be true at various times, in different places. Whatever the ambiguity of its ancestry, a good crooked knife in the hand, like a word in a well-made poem, works with its weight so balanced and shaped that it finds individual patterns of rhythm and use, intuition, invention and knowledge.

Using words to describe crooked knives accurately is difficult because the knives are nearly unclassifiable. At first glance, each knife appears simple: blade, haft, and one of four or five methods of binding blade and haft together. But blades, hafts, and bindings occur in regional, private, and natural variations. Bindings, for example, are made of cord, sinew, leather, roots, or snare wire. More elusively, the haft shape of the best knives is largely determined by the natural pattern of the grain in the wood from which it was carved. This shape follows the way root or bough met trunk or tree limb. Their intersection gives the haft its crook, one which is usually deliberately chosen to match the size and structure of the user's master hand. With yet a further turn, the crook's natural and matched-up variations are often used to inspire many theriomorphic and abstract designs. Finally, also making generalization imprecise, are misunderstandings created by English itself. *Haft, knife, blade* evoke an artifact only roughly similar in shape and largely different in use to the crooked knife.

Perhaps such difficulties explain why there are so few published descriptions. Here is one of them, from McPhee's *The Survival of the Bark Canoe*:

He then picked up his crooked knife and held its grip in his upturned right hand, the blade poking out to the left. The blade was bent near its outer end (enabling it to move in grooves and hollows where the straight part could not). Both blade and grip were shaped like nothing I had ever seen. The grip, fashioned for the convenience of a hand closing over it, was bulbous. The blade had no hinge and protruded rigidly – but not straight out. It formed a shallow V with the grip.[1]

If read quickly, the description is pleasant, fluent, and seems adequate. But when the words are read carefully in an attempt to construct the knife, they will be found to have little meaning. Whatever, for example, the clause "like nothing I had ever seen" signifies as a private accuracy, publicly it is capitulation, not definition. McPhee really offers his subject and expects of his reader a cursory empathy. Only tenuously, at least in terms of his literary style, does McPhee belong with naturalists, scientists, and travellers like Charles Waterton, Darwin, Wallace, or – at an outer chronological limit – John Muir and William Brewster. They wrote before the use of photography and specialized terminologies made literary accuracy complementary rather than prime. But there does, however, exist a more honourable modern description of the crooked knife than McPhee's, one which does belong to the tradition just noted. It appears in Adney and Chapelle's *The Bark Canoes and Skin Boats of North America*:

> It was made from a flat steel file with one side worked down to a cutting edge. The back of the blade thus formed was usually a little less than an eighth of an inch thick. The cutting edge was bevel form, like that of a drawknife or chisel, with the back face quite flat. The tang of the file was fitted into a handle made of a crotched stick, to one arm of which the tang was attached, while the other projected at a slightly obtuse angle away from the back of the blade.[2]

There is no need to make extravagant claims for this passage. Its limits are those of a certain kind of anthropological technique which concentrates upon external appearance and does not consider the cultural implications of use. But perhaps paradoxically for some readers, it is Adney and Chapelle's distanced, logical, resistant prose, rather than McPhee's fluent improvisation, which catches the instress of a crooked knife's structure. In sound as well as in accuracy their "flat steel file," "side worked down," "back of the blade thus formed," "back face quite flat" correspond to the balance and beauty of the knife with mimetic energy. Perhaps the virtue in Adney and Chapelle's words was achieved by following what Pound, talking of Hardy's poetry, described as "The old man's road ... CONTENT, the INSIDES, the subject matter."[3]

The letter from which that quotation comes was written in 1933. Just a year later *Cantos XXXI–XLI* were published. Their radical shift largely into the prosaic and historical disappointed readers who expected the lyrical mythologies of *Cantos I–XXX* to continue. For over 250 pages and nearly fourteen years following, Pound took the old man's road through America and China until he reached the *Pisan Cantos*. Reading those, one remembers the rest of the letter of 1933, for there Pound offered a second road which he simply, without further commentary, called "Music." Must there be two roads? If the *Pisan Cantos*, some moments in *The Dynasts* and Hardy's shorter poems, and even a few phrases in Adney and Chapelle's description are sufficient evidence, those two roads are one. After epistemological limits of the discursive have been reached, the old man's road may follow a way where speech, myth, and music are synonymous, a way no less real for being describable only in lesser analogies than itself. As Donne wrote: "I can see the sun in a looking-glasse, but the nature and the whole working of the Sun I cannot see in that glasse."[4]

Hold an invisible rope vertically in your master hand as if you were going to climb. Your thumb, upright, is pressed against the rope. Your fingers, clenched, circle it. Keeping fingers and thumb in place, knuckles uppermost, bring the rope to the horizontal. Press the rope upward with the ball of your thumb until a natural point of extension, rest, and resistance is reached. Your hand now holds the shape of a crooked knife's handle. Your fingers circle the straight lower part of the knife's haft into which the blade has been driven and secured by a binding. Your thumb rests in a groove carved into the underside of a wing which flares away at an obtuse angle to the lower part of the haft your fingers grip. The blade's edge faces your body. The blade cuts by being pulled toward the carver.

The form of the handle and the blade's position make the crooked knife's use an operation in which intuition and deliberation have to become indistinguishable. There are at least three points of restraint and release which play with and against one another as the knife is used. The first is the blade's contact with the wood being carved. The second is the fingers' grip on the lower haft. The third is the thumb's upward push on the underside of the obtusely angled wing of the upper haft. The fingers, in effect, work partly as a moving fulcrum, like a caesura or enjambment. They transmit and adjust effects of the thumb's pressure on the upper haft through the blade. The fingers also allow the thumb to respond to the blade's movements, giving, taking, pacing, as the blade slows or quickens and the texture of the carved wood changes.

At first, a carver familiar only with knives whose blades

are usually pushed will find the crooked knife awkward to use and dangerous. The knife insists upon the identity of user and use. It is formed to make haft and hand identical, and the blade's travel has limits which must be defined by the whole presence of the carver, not just the reach of his arm. Out of control, a pushed knife breaks clear into neutral space which has been observed by the carver, if at all, only in a casual and intermittent way. Controlled, the pulled crooked knife enters space which must be valued so carefully and continuously that it becomes part of the object being carved.

Because of this singleness of user and use, it is predictable that – like boats, cups, spoons, combs, baskets, paddles, houses, cloaks, chairs, chests, texts, and pens – all artifacts whose creation and use can be converted into ritual synecdoche, the crooked knife has often been made to bear what the Anglo-Welsh poet and painter David Jones named "sign." This is a more accurate word than "decoration" or "embellishment" since it implies synonymity of appearance and function.

Even the run of the wood's grain through the crooked knife's haft is itself sign implicit. The grain's turn at the haft's crook mounts, angled and flared, on a wing against which the carver's thumb must press. The wing is flight, flow – air and water. With four of eight knives on the table at the beginning of this essay, the makers did no more than release such natural analogies. The polishing and accidents of use, like marks of ice or the working of lichen on rock, seem to match the makers' reticences further until the knife's appearance and what the knife does have become the same.

Such tact in the making, a refusal to force the haft out of the way it once grew, is not only probably the most ancient but also the only tolerable modern way that hafts can be managed. One of the remaining four knives, the four which carry explicit signs, shows why this is true. The knife was made in New Hampshire about fifty years ago. Rising out of a large notch carved into the top of the wing of the upper part of its haft is a stack of three hearts, each heart a bit smaller than the one below it. Like most similarly naturalistic carvings of moose heads, screaming eagles, and rabbits with flattened ears, which turn up on recently made crooked knives, the hearts have the inertness of externally imposed, imperfectly understood symbolism. At best they are naive; at worst, despite the skillfulness of their carving, they are sentimental and comic.

This knife's faults become even clearer when it is compared with the crudest of the eight knives, which was made in Cape Breton about a hundred years ago. Its haft is so roughly hacked out of hardwood that nearly all the hatchet strokes can be counted. Carving on the haft consists mainly of checks and shallow grooves cut at points of finger and thumb tip pressure. On its nearly shapeless pommel, are gouged spokes of a six-armed star, which, like the stick limbs of petroglyphic figures, are more attentive to nature in its manner of operation than any realistic representation could ever be.

The Cape Breton knife, for all its crudity, is properly of the same high measure as the two knives left to be described. One has a haft of red cedar. Its flat, splayed, wedge-shaped wing is mimicked on both of its sides by continuous form lines. Around the edges of its upper surface are incised margins of triangular crenellations. Across the angle formed by the knife's upper and lower haft is carved the smooth, finned hump of a breaching killer whale, leviathan, looking as though it were swimming down the haft to enter what the blade carves. The second crooked knife, Cherokee, has a haft of black walnut with a crook that rises and tightens into a spiraling, layered hub whose coils seem to be constantly adjusting themselves with a motion that is really minutely proportioned stasis. A snake, perhaps a northern black racer (*Coluber constrictor*), a quick glittering blackness, braided. But it is also ouroboros, the serpent ring of eternity, "everything issuing from everything, depending on everything, and connecting with everything."[5] It is kundalini, Mercurius, twined around the tree of earth out of which it has been made and within which it still lives. The haft of this Cherokee knife both is and enacts the play and ply of form as outward shape and of form as an essential, determinant principle; of the created and uncreated; of *natura naturata* and *natura naturans*, which, as Donne stated, "the understanding of man cannot comprehend."[6] It contains all eight knives and none. It both is and is not all the makers and users of knives and their making and use, for as the *Tao Tê Ching* says, "the greatest cutting does not sever."[7]

When Edmund Carpenter wrote about Inuit perception of language and use, it was with similar analogies: "Words are like the knife of the carver: they free the idea, the thing, from the general formlessness of the outside. As a man speaks, not only is his language in a state of birth, but also the very thing about which he is talking."[8] Those who use the knife face the formless. They also are the form they face.

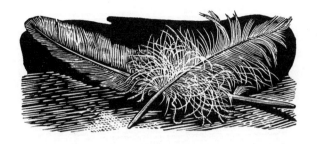

Keeping: The Cameron Yard

As master of a vessel and sailing up to the Cameron Yard for the first time on a spring tide in October 1885, you could have read this:

SHUBENACADIE RIVER

The entrance to this river which is on the South side of Cobequid Bay near its head, lies East-Southerly about 13 miles from Burntcoat Head Lighthouse, and Southeasterly 6½ miles from Spencer Point Lighthouse ... Mean rise and fall of Tides, 48 feet. This is the highest rise in the Bay of Fundy.[1]

Those directions come from *Eldridge's Coast Pilot, No. 1, Eastern Section* (Boston, 1884). Eldridge's *Pilot* might have been wedged on a shelf in your cabin by the side of another necessary book, one of the many editions of Nathaniel Bowditch's *New American Practical Navigator: Being An Epitome of Navigation Containing All the Tables Necessary To Be Used With The Nautical Almanac In Determining The Latitude, And The Longitude By Lunar Observations And Keeping A Complete Reckoning At Sea* ..., and so on, for nineteen more lines of a title page which was nothing if not inclusive. Inclusive also was the owner of my copy of Bowditch's *Navigator*, a fourteenth edition published in 1844. He wrote on its flyleaf: "James Foot, Pictou, N.S., July 3rd, 1858," adding for absolute surety, "His Booke."

But neither books of navigation nor navigators can afford to be inconclusive. Perhaps children have the same sense of what is at issue when they end ownership inscriptions in their schoolbooks with "the world, the universe." And since on that October day, on a rising tide in 1885, you now face a run up the Shubenacadie River of about five miles to the Cameron Yard, and since you must make this run up one of the most actively tidal rivers in the world, filling and falling through nearly fifty feet, and since you must gauge a safe distance to catch the highest water and not catch up with a tidal bore cresting ahead, blocking the river's outfalling current with a rush of four or five knots, you might also want to turn from Eldridge's *Pilot* to a section of inclusive Bowditch headed "Evolutions at Sea" and read this note "On a Ship's Driving":

When it happens that there is not sufficient room to work in a tide's way, through a crowd of ships, or in a narrow channel, but that the ship must drive by the help of the tide, it may be done, provided the tide be strong enough in proportion to the wind. This art consists in keeping the ship in a fair way, by a management of rudder and the sails.[2]

Therefore, "it may be done." And can you do it? Whatever else may be involved, it is a case of drive or be driven.

What else can be made of such a passage? In one way, there is the obvious reading that can easily be restated. Running up the Shubenacadie in a hull which displaces water rather than planing on top of it can only be safely done if the hull moves either at the same speed or slightly more slowly than the tidal current it follows. If the hull is driven by the wind more quickly than the current flows, its bow will dig into the water and its stern slew. Then the hull will set sideways to the current, become unsteerable, and possibly even capsize.

In a second way of reading, Bowditch's words provoke psychological reconstruction and self-reflection. As a ship's master reading them in 1885, how would you have reacted? Would you have felt sardonic irritation at Bowditch's self-sufficient cogency? Or would you have felt a faith in yourself confirmed by Bowditch's assumption that what "may be done" you could do?

There is a third way of reading Bowditch's words, one to which we are less directly driven than to the former two. You would rather drive, though you are not now master of that ship in October, 1885, not now sailing it past the village of Maitland (to starboard, at the river's mouth) where eleven years before W. D. Lawrence had launched from his yard the ship named after himself which was, at 2,459 tons, he claimed, the largest ever built in Canada. Now, you will never steer by Black Rock (to port), past Eagle's Nest Point (to port) and Big Plaster Rock Quarry (to starboard) between two-hundred-foot-high cliffs of red sandstone, limestone, and shale shot through with veins of gypsum. Now, you are almost completely released from the real context of Bowditch's words (it seems). Your desperations are not the immediate ones of wind and water and matching them both to arrive at the Cameron Yard. You are in fact there at the Yard already. You are here, in a place not yet clearly identified or described, carrying with you perhaps from Bowditch only this much, these words released from the context of his time and taken over into our time: "This art consists in keeping ... in a fair way, by a management ..."

What lies in our keeping here? At the simplest, this: between 1880 and 1894, William P. Cameron built eight vessels in the Cameron Yard in South Maitland. They were the *Isabel, Eva Maud, Linnet, Selkirk, Savona, Canadian* (later named *Ensenada*), *Kathleen Hilda,* and *Edith.* Of the four largest, the first, the *Isabel*, was a barque of 1,260 tons, launched in 1880. Two others were true ships, rigged with square sails on each of at least three masts. They were the *Selkirk*, 1,757 tons, launched in 1886, and the *Savona*, 1,659 tons, launched in 1891. The fourth large vessel was the 1,072-ton, four-masted barquentine *Canadian* or *Ensenada*, rigged with square sails on her foremast, fore and aft sails elsewhere. She was launched in 1889. The smallest and logically the last Cameron vessel was the steam schooner *Edith*, 45 tons, launched in 1894. Her sails probably served as an economical auxiliary to the speed, reliability, and maneuverability offered by her engine. She must have been the issue of Cameron's attempts to keep up with changes in patterns of trade and in technology.

We know something of what these vessels looked like. Not only does the record of their types – barque, barquentine, ship, and so on – indicate how they were rigged, but also some pictures exist. An oil painting of the *Isabel* hangs in the old Lawrence house in Maitland. It shows her running before a gale with most of her sails furled. She is painted white, as white as the crests on the wave scuds which make a grid of static violence all around her. The sheer of her bow is as sleek as the chine of a salmon. Also to have survived is a set of photographs which shows not a Cameron vessel but the *Calburga*, a 1,406-ton, three-masted barque, built by Adam McDougall and registered in South Maitland in 1890. She was a blockier vessel than the *Isabel*, black hulled. It is pleasant to think (on insufficient grounds) that all the Cameron vessels were characterized by fine lines. F. W. Wallace, the naval historian, found the *Calburga* in Digby, Nova Scotia, in 1913 when she was loading a cargo of deals for Buenos Aires. He took photographs of her, including her deck work, which show the careful beading, trim, Palladian ornamentation, capping, coping, and balustrade work of the poop deck, cabin trunk, and aft companionway. The craftsmen who did this work may also have been among those who worked on the Cameron vessels. The *Calburga* foundered off the Irish coast during the First World War. She was the last Canadian-built square-rigger of substantial size still registered in Canada.[3]

How are we to read what else is left? There are some stories. There are also some names whose own defining stories have vanished, leaving the names at the mercy of present interest, assimilation, or appropriation. One story concerns Wilson, second mate on the *Savona*. He was nearly murdered during a voyage from Calcutta to Bombay. An Austrian seaman tried to stab him with a sheath knife. Wilson caught the knife's blade in his bare hands, snapped it off at the haft. Drive or be driven. And there is this story, really without a name, current still in local hearsay, about a daughter of Cameron's, young, in her teens, tossed from her riding horse and killed while riding down the road to the river and Yard.

And there are names without stories. In a nearby graveyard

of what is now the United and was once the Presbyterian church – a squarish, steepleless, clapboarded, white-painted, snug little building, trim as a dough box – there are three related headstones. One reads:

In Memory of Annie
dau of William & Abbie Cameron
died Nov. 28, 1870
Ae 1 yr. & 3 ms
Safe on the bosom of thy God
Fair Spirit rest thee now
Tho' here on earth thy stay was short
His seal was on thy brow.

The second stone bears a flower carved at its crest, a rose perhaps, almost erased by weathering. Its inscription reads:

Flora
dau of W. P. & Abbie Cameron
died Feb. 28, 1875
aged 5 mo's.

The third is a double stone, a diptych. Its serrated crest is divided into two pinnacles with a common valley between. Each pinnacle caps a column of lettering surmounted by a carving depicting a recumbent lamb. The left column reads:

Jessie
died June 7, 1880
Aged 1 yr. & 8 mo's.

The right reads:

Innis
died June 3, 1880
Aged 3 yrs. & 5 mo's.

Running across the bottom of the stone beneath both columns
is lettered:

Children of W. P. & Abbie Cameron
Sleep on sweet babes and take your rest
God called you home he thought it best.

Are those stones also part of Bowditch's "art … in keeping a
fair way, by a management …"? W. P. Cameron launched the
first of his vessels, the barque *Isabel*, in the year of the last and
double burial. Had he heard a saying favoured by W. D. Law-
rence, the great shipbuilder in Maitland, at the mouth of the
river, who was to die in 1886: "Kites rise against, not with the
wind"? After Cameron sold the Yard, it is said that he went to

California. Perhaps one can rightly guess some reasons why he chose not to finish where he began. Ortega y Gasset wrote: "When we stand before the universe unmoved by any personal interest we see nothing well."[4] His words imply an antithetical corollary: we may be moved, and must see the universe only too well.

Somewhere between the stories with names and the names without stories is something else to consider. There exists a photograph, undated, untitled, but clearly taken at the Cameron Yard because the shape of the river's banks, the cut of an entering creek, the white patch of exposed limestone deposit in the river cliff to the south of the Yard have softened, slipped, and shifted over the years only enough to make them still recognizably similar to older appearance. In the photograph, what is now forest and intervale marsh is cleared land. The photograph's ground is covered with short, rough grass, spattered by what appear to be white chips of gypsum. In the river, a tugboat is either pushing a small barge to shore or preparing to pull it clear. Smoke from the tug's caricaturally tall and narrow stack drifts an arrested plume southerly, probably driven by that north wind which always comes with an inflowing tide. On the bank are two buildings. One is a small, peak-roofed shed sided with vertical rough planks. The other is a square, horizontally-planked structure. It seems to be flat-topped. A ladder-runged derrick projects out of the structure, slung on a balance of guying cables. To the left side of the photograph, watching the tug, is a group of five women. They wear dark, heavy-looking skirts which reach the ground, white shirt waists and wide-brimmed hats with thickly ribboned or massively floral crowns. Each woman slants a parasol across her shoulder. Standing in the centre of the photograph is a horse. Behind it trails a loose drag rope. The horse hangs its head low, from hunched shoulders, as if the horse collar it wears is burden enough for any horse to have to bear.

The scene in this photograph has the same kind of calculated tensive repose as a Seurat painting. A granular stipple suffuses the photograph's surface and makes uncertain the time of day when it was taken. No one and nothing seem to cast shadows. Their time is an arrested, overcast noon of forever. You wait for the parasols to spin and pose new angles reflecting a flash of silk from the invisible sun. You wait for the tug's smoke to drift farther south, thinning into haze. You wait for the righteous horse to lift its head and shake its harness with a sound of flapped leather and slipped lines. You wait for the photograph's world to break loose in movement, colour, and noise; and nothing happens but the intense, silent exclusion the photograph insists upon, seemingly shadowless.

By saying "seemingly," one acknowledges shadows which must be there. Without shadows there can be no images. One's language, technical knowledge, feeling, and immediate perception shift from the facts of the photograph to a metaphorical extension of those facts and back to the photograph's facts again in such a situation, trying both to accommodate and con-tradict the cast of repression which inflects the photograph's images. But what are really repressed in the photograph are past and future. The photograph's antiquity and atemporality are deceptions. Its time is wholly present. For us, its subject may seem to be past, but that assumption contradicts the truism that no static, spatial re-presentation can re-present the past, which is always time passing. The apparent permanence of the photograph's images is an immediate present which we, living really in historical time, cannot enter. The physical sub-stance of the photograph, the condition of the paper upon which it was printed, the chemistry of its surface, these can enter time in various states of deterioration and preservation. But the photograph's images cannot do so, at least not without our help. Like a language, like a poem, like the meaning of the words "Cameron Yard," the images in the photograph of Cameron Yard are in our keeping. Either we make them appropriate (if never fully adequate) signs of what they pur-port to show, or we allow them to rest in mere presentness. If the latter happens, the photograph becomes only an object. If it is used at all at any more complex level than that of subjec-tive, sentimental self-projection, it is judged by a deracinated aesthetic of form and found adequate to canon, or wanting. For many of us, the verses the Camerons chose for the graves of their dead children have become such objects.

Now, the time is October. It is usually too awkward and

too dangerous in that month of this century to come to the Cameron Yard by river. Even if you did, no wharf stands to receive you. Though the old books of pilotage still fit in principle, they do not deal with new channels and shifted sandbars. The "White Square building with lantern on top" which Eldridge noted "at this date (1884)" as showing a "fixed White Light" at Black Rock, on the south side entrance to the Shubenacadie, is no longer there. Neither is the place where the photographer set up equipment to take the picture of Cameron Yard. Among the spruce, maples, birch, alders, poplars, and apple trees which now cover the north side of the Yard is no elevation where a camera could have been placed to account for the photograph's angle. An explanation which does account for it is that the photographer stood on the deck of a vessel still shore bound on building stocks. The camera looked out some thirty or forty feet high from what now is air and once was a place that went to sea. As a navigator would put it, present position doubtful.

Now, the time is October. Leaves are becoming what you expect them to become but are always confounded by. Yellow light in the birch and poplar or red and yellow light in the maples pulls you up through balancing colour into somewhere inside you outside, lifting away. This is a place to walk not on eggs but on apples where old trees have tipped up their roots to lean an elbow on earth. Your clothing flecks with points of fluff where seeds ride, and in the old fields

48

of drying goldenrod, grasshoppers flick themselves free and rattle clear.

For nearly two years, three or four times a week, I have walked this way to the Cameron Yard. When I started, most of the way was a game trail. In two years, I have made it into a path. Before my walking and before the recent walking and running of deer, foxes, raccoons, rabbits, and squirrels, parts of this way to the Cameron Yard were called the Plaster Road. It carried wagons loaded with gypsum, hauled down from a quarry on the ridge above the river. The gypsum was loaded onto scows at the Cameron Yard's wharf. Before the nineteenth-century road, there must have been other variations on the same ground, built and travelled by the Scots, who were granted land there after the American Revolutionary War, and before them by the Acadians, who were expelled before the Scots arrived. Before the Acadians, a Mi'kmaq path and earlier game trails probably defined where later roads and my own path were to follow.

About eight years ago, I wrote an essay in which there was a poet who persuaded me to walk such roads. Perhaps he was thinking of Alistair MacLeod's road to Rankins' Point, Charles Bruce's Mulgrave Road, Ernest Buckler's unnamed, unnameable road up the South Mountain of the Annapolis Valley, or Douglas Lochhead's High Marsh Road across the Tantramar. Or, he could have been thinking of unliterary roads he might have travelled, the signs for which I have also seen: Rabbittown Road, Lintlop Road, Salem Loop, Rock Road. That poet on the Biorachan Road had a mind of his own. I chose the thoughts of someone else to walk with me now. Call him Meton and remember the "Let Meton speak" of John Thompson's Ghazal xx, and his original, the Meton in Letter cxii of Walter Savage Landor's epistolary novel *Pericles and Aspasia*, who is "no prompt debater, no acute logician, no clear expositor." Merton was an astronomer. He could have told me if earth is the ash of a fallen star. Later, his was to be a natural block of limestone whose central fissure points to the circuit of Ursa Major.

We began together where the Plaster Road has been almost elided with forest. Fifty-foot-high columns of spruce, four-feet thick at the butt, grow from the road's sunken crown. Alder splays spring lodged branches across all other space. Walking is dodging and ducking, lifting and holding down and kneeling sometimes to crawl in the road's trough of green moss. From mid-summer on through fall, orange, yellow, white, brown, even black mushrooms play puckfist and push out of that moss. In summer, the light beneath the great trees is greened by moss and feathers of spruce, and living inside it is like hanging head down, looking down into steeps of a leaf-stained lake where banks of elodea cast sunlight in their colour.

This submarine part of the Plaster Road ends at the old boundary of the Cameron Yard, Cameron Creek. The Creek's bed is a fault, from twenty to a hundred feet deep, running back into the face of the escarpment which parallels the river's course. Slabs of sedimentary limestone, fissuring in thin flat plates, tip out of the fault's sides. Everywhere there are signs of sliding, slipping pressures, of the earth having been fractured, tilted, almost having lost hold of its bedrock but hanging on, hauling back.

Over this creek the Plaster Road lofts itself onto a vanished trestle bridge of logs and squared timbers. A few weeks ago, after Meton left, I found all that remains of the bridge. I was climbing about in the Creek's almost dry bed when I saw a wet stain of oxide, reddish, in a pocket of rock. Underneath the oxide's skin were the eroded stubs of three iron spikes, about one inch in diameter, which had been rolled into a crevice by the force of the Creek's spring and fall freshets. The last voice of iron is rust. Those stubs were nearly ten yards downstream from the point where the old bridge finally fell to be torn apart by water and thrown into the Shubenacadie.

Beyond that invisible bridge, the Plaster Road disappears among trees, weeds, and bushes which cover the north side of what was Cameron's Yard. The whole Yard must once, in a sense, have been a road. The Plaster Road simply entered a ten-acre expansion of itself made of cleared, ditched, tamped-down woodland and marsh. Among all the present obscuring growth in the old Yard, it is the wild apple trees which are most apparent now, with their green, yellow, and red fruit hanging on that ultimate stem of stillness which one tap of wind can shake from the bough. A language almost extinct – one which used, needed, and delighted in such distinctions – called these kinds of trees "wildings." As wildings, the trees are also keepings, for their fruit carries the sign of more civil scions: MacIntosh, Starr, Roxbury Russet, Fall Pippin, Gravenstein, and King. All the poems worth reading are wildings.

A hundred years ago when you came into the Cameron Yard on the Plaster Road, you would have seen the originals of those wildings planted close to the buildings which then were there. To your left, by the riverside, were the stocks and scaffoldings, probably with a partly finished hull resting upon blocks, its stern square to the river. After frost or a light scatter of early snow, I have seen a quick, warm sun melt into the earth where the stocks stood a series of parallel lines about two or three yards apart, which shows where the bed logs carrying the weight of the hull and stocks were half buried. After leaves fall and weeds die back, you can also see that the earth has been dug out into a shallow, ship-shaped depression some sixty feet wide by five hundred long. Ditches run down both sides of the depression. Also on both sides of it are bowl-shaped holes into which props were driven to hold up the hulls. At one side of this ship-shaped depression, near the river, is a small pile of fire-stained stones which were part of a forge's construction. The pile is now almost hidden by spruce. Where the roots of one tree grow along and above the ground before slipping under, half a dozen foot-long forged iron spikes are laid in a row. Their heads are tilted up by the growing root as if they were still being offered to the hand which put them down.

To your right, if you had entered the Cameron Yard on the Plaster Road a hundred years ago, you would have seen the cookhouse. Now it is only a cellar filled with goldenrod or snow or seep water, as the season determines, and by a birch whose multiple trunks lift out of one great, squat bole. The cellar's walls have been pinched in, undermined and tumbled by frost and by the saps of water and shifting soil. The cellar is slowly levelling itself up with the surrounding ground. A neighbour told me how he played in the cookhouse while it still stood fifty years ago. Its floors tilted then and made him run and slide over them as if he were, as he said, in the world of a crazy mirror. He remembered the cookhouse being still filled with crockery. Now there remains in one corner of the cellar a shattered half cup, white porcelain, with ears of wheat braided around its rim. Scooped in the moss it seems midway to the lips of the man who stooped there to take a supple drink of soil.

Apart from these remnants of stocks and cookhouse, little else is left of the Cameron Yard. At the very edge of the river are three logs, almost completely buried, set at right angles to the bank and projecting over it by several ice-scarred inches. Probably they are hemlock. Only that wood could have survived for so long. As the old people say, hemlock kept wet never rots. Upon those logs, Cameron Yard's wharf was built. Another set of embedded logs lies two hundred paces back from the river, on land which has broken free of trees to revert to intervale marsh covered with spartina grass. Iron spikes three feet long protrude from these logs. Perhaps they were a foundation for the boilers which powered the Yard's sawmill and provided steam for the steam box where planks and small framing members were bent into shape.

One other place remains. Behind the cookhouse cellar, on a knoll whose south side looks out upon the Yard below and whose north side drops sheer one hundred feet into the fault of Cameron Creek, is a graveyard. Its original extent has disappeared beneath the growing trees. Spruce grow in and around it. Only one lettered stone makes it recognizable as a graveyard at all. The other marks are intuitable as memorials because of the lettered stone's presence among them. They are small slabs of limestone, sunk vertically and almost completely so that only the rim of each juts above the layers of spruce needles. The lettered stone is marble. It has been snapped off its base and leans against a spruce tree's trunk. Its inscription reads:

In Memory of
William Cameron
Died July 1830
Aged 56 Y'rs

Also His Wife
Mary Cameron
died May 7, 1868
Aged 85 Yrs.

Which Camerons are these? Mary Cameron was born in 1793, her husband, William, in 1774. He was too young to have held the first grant of this land after the American Revolution. Was he the first owner's son? Were the Camerons, William and Mary, William P. Cameron's parents or (it is possible) grandparents? How did they live? Was the Yard, in an earlier part of its existence, the site of a succession of two, perhaps three, Cameron farms? Was there a house, were there houses where the cookhouse cellar now slowly fills with earth? Who else is buried on the knoll, marked by those limestone slabs? Upon how many layers of fact and meaning is a civilization built, even one as short as that which took its fall at the Cameron Yard? Are the layers as many as the years lived by those who created it? Is that civilization still falling? "This art consists in keeping … in a fair way, by a management." If those words are meaningless now, it has fallen. If they are not, certain acts and re-enactments are possible. As Auden wrote: "Man is an analogy-making animal; that is his great good fortune."[5] Or, as Emerson said in Chapter IV of *Nature*: "… man is an analogist, and studies relations in all objects. He is placed in the centre of beings, and a ray of relation passes from every other being to him. And neither can man be understood without these objects, nor these objects without man." Drive or be driven. Understand, or be misunderstood.

Early last spring, not far from the graveyard knoll, I heard the sound of water forced over a spillway. Through a gap in the trees that faces east toward the river I saw for a moment the white head, dark body, and white tail of an adult bald eagle flying south toward the Cameron Yard. The noise of water spilling was made by leaves on a four-foot bough the eagle carried crosswise in its talons. The latest provisional dominance in the Yard is that of the eagles. A pair has nested for several years in the flat crown of a battered white pine which grows from the side of a cliff rising on the south margin of the Yard's marsh intervale. To get close to the eyrie quickly and easily is impossible. The cliff and its pine are separated from the Yard's portion of intervale marsh by a tidal creek which is uncrossable, except by boat, at any point but three quarters of a mile up its course, where it ceases to be tidal. Apart from its flat crown, the eyrie pine is nearly bare. Only two or three thinly needled plateaus of bough grow from the upper half of its trunk. The eyrie is far larger than anything the tree has visibly grown. It is like a wadded tangle of tree roots, like the whole ball of root ripped up when wind tips an old tree over.

For nearly two years, I have watched this eyrie. Always but once, I have watched only from among the trees on the distant north side of the Yard. The adults have raised two broods of two eaglets each during that time. The one contradiction I made to keeping the width of the whole interval between me and the eyrie happened during August of the first year. I thought all the birds had gone hunting on the tidal flats and walked to the near bank of the tidal creek to a point opposite the pine and the cliff. Then I watched as a sack-like broken stump on a low dead limb on the pine slowly became the sullen, fuscous hunch of an eaglet, hiding from me, hating and fearing me. I walked away, trying to tell the eaglet by means of my carriage that I did not know it was there and that its immobility had worked. Eagles, unlike chickadees, seem to have little interest in comedy.

It was to see the eagles, their young, and their eyrie from the right distance that I brought Meton over the Plaster Road to the Cameron Yard two months ago. As soon as we crossed Cameron Creek, we could hear eagles screaming. Far off they sound like screaming gulls. But heard close, those screams are the sound of breath overdriven and split on beveled, living bone. Like ancient music, their screams are pentatonic, absolute, unanswerable except on their own terms. Meton and I stopped at the edge of the trees where the interval begins. Five hundred yards south of us, across the marsh, across the uncrossable tidal creek, standing on the narrow strip of intervale at the base of the cliff where the eyrie pine grows were two men. They wore dun-coloured clothes. Each carried a video camera. They stepped toward the cliff and backed away from it, trying angles, the cameras held up to their faces almost continuously as if seeing anything in any other way were impossible. Meton and I could make out one of the eaglets standing at the base of the main bough supporting the eyrie. It was as still and as silent as the eaglet I had insulted the year before. The two adult eagles were screaming. One eagle was just coming in from down river, flying in low and screaming in answer to the other, which was half-flying, half-jumping from treetop to treetop. One of the dun men lowered his camera, looked down to find new footing in the mud, turned to find better and saw us. He must have spoken to the other. Both faced us. Meton and I waited for the cameras to lift and be directed at us.

Of course, the cameras were not. We did not fit the pattern those dun men had in mind. We were awkwardly present witnesses. For them, we should not exist. We were not meant to be there. In truth, we really did have no legal permission or authority to be in the Cameron Yard, let alone on the adjacent property south of it, where they stood. They, on the other hand, may have had such right. Their uniform of dun-coloured clothes argued as much. As they looked at us briefly before turning back to filming, the dun men must have decided on a non-existence for us like the one they planned for themselves in the final filmed scheme of eagles they were aiming to show. The dun men had not, therefore, crossed the creek three quarters of a mile up its course. They were not standing at the base of the cliff where the pine lofted an eyrie. The eagles were not frightened and angered by them because the dun men were not there.

What was there? An abstraction called "nature" whose specifics were "eagles"? A scripted present, appropriated in camera (since Meton and I were not there)? A parody of what might be called a form of real presence? For no doubt a dun-coloured reverence was involved, though the eagles did not think so. As I write this and read a way into it, I think of how Auden qualified the words quoted earlier in this essay. He wrote: "Man is an analogy-drawing animal; that is his great good fortune." The qualification adds "His danger is of treating analogies as identities, for instance, 'Poetry should be as much like music as possible.' I suspect that the people who are most likely to say this are the tone deaf. The more one loves an art, the less likely it is that one will wish to trespass upon its domain." We all know the kind of people, the mad, the foolish, the incapable, Auden is after. But we may also know some who are none of these. We may know those who can see and hear the play of logic, form, and feeling common to both music and poetry, for whom words and tones, script and sound are not different but only alternative codes. For the latter listeners and speakers, what Auden calls "identities," the specifics of an art, are defined by all available analogies. Some might name this play of identity and analogy – in which each of the two exchanges its place with the other so swiftly that neither ever settles as the other – a myth, and mean by that word either nothing or all. What then is the Cameron Yard – analogy or identity? And where must we place Bowditch's words: "This art consists in keeping ... in a fair way, by a management"? Are not all our arts and acts navigations? What were the eagles screaming? Identity or analogy? For the dun men really neither, though one might guess they came close to considering those screams identities of merely a rightless, nearly meaningless kind. What is clearer is that for dun men, eagles scream in no empyrean, although other humans have thought otherwise. There is, for example, this in the fourth chapter of *Revelation*: "... the first beast was like a lion, and the second beast like a calf, and the third beast had a face as a man and the fourth beast was like a flying eagle." Are those beasts analogies or identities? I do not just speak of the traditional conversions to Mark, Luke, Matthew, and John, the last being the "flying eagle," Dante's *"aguglia di Cristo."* For are those beasts not involved in a ceaseless exchange of analogy and identity which is both myth and life?

The eagles screaming at Cameron Yard can lead to a myth (or life) which accords with the sense being tried here. In Canto XVIII of the *Paradiso*, Dante ascends to the sixth sphere, governed by Jupiter, and sees the spirits of the just singing "in sheaths of living light," moving to form a script of light which spells, *"Diligite justitiam qui judicatis terram."* In English, the Latin means "Love justice, you who judge the earth."[6] Its source is one of the apocryphal gospels, the first chapter, first verse of *The Wisdom of Solomon*. Dante watches the spirits of the just:

> In five times seven vowels and consonants
>> they showed themselves, and I grasped every part
>> as if those lights had given it utterance.

The translation used here is John Ciardi's. Like, I am sure, many other modern readers, Ciardi seems to be discomfited by this moment in Dante's vision. At least discomfiture is betrayed by the annotation he offers on the passage just quoted: "I do not know why hearing a letter spoken should make it [more] 'graspable' than seeing it flash across the sky, but Dante, a primitive art critic at best, was always filled with awe by the sort of visual presentation that seemed to make the viewer hear what he was seeing."[7] Incomprehension here is nicely balanced by condescension. The reply to both is that Dante was a poet. The identity of his art and the analogical form of script in which it was coded were indistinguishable for him within the myth and life he found and was given. In a sermon alluding to Psalm 19 Donne similarly thought: "How often does the Holy Ghost call upon us, in the Scriptures, *Ecce, quia os Domini locutum*, Behold, the mouth of the Lord hath spoken it? He calls us to *behold*, (which is the office of the *eye*) and that we are to behold, is the *voice* of God, belonging to the eare; seeing is hearing, in God's first language, the language of *works*."[8] Donne's limitations also, of course, were poetic and primitive, as were those of the sonnet maker who wrote, "To hear with eyes belongs to love's fine wit."

The spirits of the just in the *Paradiso*'s Canto xviii continue to the next seeing and hearing in a logical way, contradicting again present neutral notions of language, by transforming themselves and the "*m*" in *terram*, the earth of living light, into an imperial eagle of light which, throughout the rest of Canto xviii and in Cantos xix and xx, speaks and sings to Dante (and us) about divine justice, which it both is and signifies, of which it is both the identity and analogy.

> What I must now call back from memory
> > No voice has ever spoken, nor ink written.
> > Nor has its like been known to fantasy.
>
> For I saw and heard the beak move and declare
> > in its own voice the pronouns "I" and "mine"
> > When "we" and "ours" were what conceived it there.[9]

No doubt for the dun men in Cameron Yard, as for Ciardi, seeing was seeing, not seeing and hearing, not hearing and understanding the eagles' screams. But, admittedly, seeing is there for the taking. It could be all you, rather than we, get in the end. And Meton? Meton did not speak. He shared a mouth to be torn at the tripod. We went back the way we had come, past the site of the stocks where the *Isabel*, *Linnet*, *Selkirk*, *Savona*, *Ensenada* and the other vessels were built, past the site of the cookhouse cellar with its single shattered cup, past the graveyard knoll which we did not visit this time, for we had seen and heard what we could, and each of us had other keepings and reckonings to manage.

Groundmass

Neither spherical nor spheroid, it might still be as close as I will ever come to lifting that "great ball of crystal / ... the great acorn of light" in Pound's Canto cxvi.[1] I found it in an old, splayed, galvanized sheet-metal shed which was garage to the farmhouse my wife and I bought fourteen years ago. At the back of this shed was an oil-sodden, wooden workbench, and beneath that, in a litter of gravel, black sawdust, and rotten shavings, it struck partially through as a dusty glistening.

After I had pried it loose, it became a slab of rock, two inches thick, roughly the size and shape of a large hand held palm upward with fingers extended. I washed it in the creek which flows through the centre of our upper hayfield, and its surface sluiced clear into a vitreous, silvery-white translucence. It looked like crystal quartz. But it was soft. I could mark it with my thumbnail. And there were layerings visible along its edges, laminations, to the eye several hundred at least within its two-inch thickness, and they were divided into groupings of fifty or so by black, threadline bands above and below. As the flowing stream rinsed it, the surface of this rock became itself like a static skin of water, one which was furled, rivelled, and striated like the skim as a sea wave lays itself over sand at the furthermost reach of its motion, just before draining back.

Fourteen years ago I knew almost nothing about this rock, or much about any other rock for that matter. I did know that rocks were mainly an obstacle to be dealt with in circumstances which, at best, only tried your patience, at worst, were exhausting and sometimes dangerous. I had cleared rocks from old fields to plant some small crop of vegetables. I had repaired old, rock-walled basements and house foundations. I had hauled rock to fill potholes in roads and tracks and used it to rebuild washed-out culvert sluiceways and stream banks. I knew something about what I could lever, lift, or roll into place on crude axles of logs. I knew about the movement of rock in frost and thaw and how the surrounding groundmass can act like the sea, turn a rock buoyant and, over the course of years, toss it up to the topsoil surface like a keg of air. But all this experience had been among the granite glacial deposits and conglomerates of the Cobequid Mountains fifty miles or so north of where I found the glistening nameless rock in a galvanized metal shed on an old farm in South Maitland whose fields and woods shelved down toward the Shubenacadie River.

Of course I could easily have found someone with enough geology to give the rock a scientific name. I could also have looked the rock up as soon as I found it in some elementary field guide to minerals, one of those with photographs categorized by colour as if rocks were birds. Later, when I knew more, I was to use such a field guide in the same spirit as you happily confirm the correct answer to a mathematical problem by reworking its solution backwards. But back then I remembered a sentence of Coleridge's I admired enough to have put in a notebook: "The shortest way gives me *knowledge* best, but the longest makes me more *knowing*."[2] Fourteen years ago, in a new marriage, in a new old house on an old property, with new words to find and learn to speak, I shied from the shortest way. Old houses are like old poems. Over time, you can hope to discover in both something laid away and left behind from someone else's life that recovers part of your own. If you are lucky and patient enough to find such a thing, you may have of love its right intelligence. Such a thing the rock seemed it might prove to be; and there might be at least as many ways of knowing it as there were of naming it correctly. Perhaps knowing and naming could even prove to be the same. Perhaps a laminar language would have to be involved, a language evolved over time, a language of ground mass, not ground zero.

There are precedents. In the summer of 1842, for example, Dr. Harding of Kentville and Mr. Pryor of Horton accompanied Charles Lyell (1797–1875), Anglo-Scot, author of *The Principles of Geology* (Volume One, 1830; Volume Two, 1832; Volume Three, 1833), out onto the tidal red mud flats of the Bay of Fundy at Wolfville, Kings County, Nova Scotia. "The red mud had cracked," wrote Lyell, "in hardening in the sun's heat, and was divided into compartments, as we see clay at the bottom of a dried pond." Dr. Harding, Mr. Pryor, and the shortly to be Sir Charles Lyell dug up one of those compartments intact as if they were lifting a cement paving stone. On its upper surface, six footprints of a least sandpiper (*Tringa minutilla*), known sometimes in Nova Scotia as a sandy pipe, were inscribed. Lyell split the slab horizontally along a laminar seam. "I was fortunate enough to lay open an under surface, on which two other lines of foot-prints appeared in relief ... These are the casts of impressions which had been made on an inferior layer deposited several tides before; and I ascertained that on the upper and under surfaces of several other thin laminae ... there exist similar foot-marks, each set made by birds at different times." Lyell took the sandy pipe slabs back to England, presenting them to the British Museum "in order that those naturalists who are still very skeptical as to the real origin of ancient fossil ornithicnites ... may compare the fossil products of the month of July, 1842, with those referable to feathered bipeds which preceded the Icthyosaurus, Iguanodon and Pterodactly."[3] As far as I know, that was the first time Nova Scotian sandpipers were accorded what can, in retrospect, be called international literary attention. The second time was in the era of the Sherman tank and the Flying Fortress when a sandpiper skeltered across the beach at Lockeport, Shelburne County, Nova Scotia, in August, 1946 to join the memory of a sandpiper on a beach in Florida in 1937 and like "a student of Blake" (like Northrop Frye) became, I believe, part of a poem by Elizabeth Bishop.

Bishop's sandpiper is bemused. But sandpipers always know what they are about. By August, their intents are Brazilian. Their apparently aimless, finicky dither is a manner of looking at the world like a poet, obliquely, with a certain accuracy and adequacy. You might call it a matter of natural manners. And the sandpipers of July, 1842, were no more out of place on red Fundy mud and in the attentions of Lyell's prose than the sandpiper on Lockeport Beach in August, 1946 is in a poem which Bishop called (with the complex, ironic rectitude of all the titles she chose) "Sandpiper," as if a simple tune about sand were all she had had time to write. For Lyell's prose and Bishop's poem, despite their apparent dissimilarities of moment, purpose, and manner, are both occasions of the real, not the nominal, and both are animate with the spirit of analogy.

Enemies of analogical meaning are various and can be nimbly diffusive, but in general they resolve into one of three categories. Paradoxically those in the first of the categories are the least obstructive, although they are usually the most dismissive. For them a sandpiper is a sandpiper. They take the real in their own way. For them, poetry is not real, most of the time, except when they write it. At least many of them have seen sandpipers; and if they come across Bishop's poem they afterwards watch the shore with increased affection. More obstructive are those in the second category who cannot tell a sandpiper from a sanderling and have no intention of ever being able to do so. For them the minute particulars, the taxonomy of detail which defines identity, difference, and thus the exactitude and energy of analogy, are matters of indifference. They live in a generalizable world. Theirs is not an indifference Bishop shared. Her trip to Sable Island in 1946 was made, among other reasons, to meet an Ipswich sparrow. The third category of those who inhibit analogical meaning are the most dangerous to it. They appear to concede it full value, but in practice keep analogy within the limits of the discursive and non-poetic. As critics and readers they often handle poems as if poetry were the criminal, conspiratorial artifact of a language which must be interrogated into the explanations of sociology, economics, psychology, or similar disciplines, into anything else, that is, but the meaning, sound, and movement of words in a particular poem which has been made in a world of many other poems. Characteristically, interpretations of the third category (which often unconsciously draw upon the resources of the first and second categories) are never quite wrong, but never wholly right. Their wrongness is the result of not knowing, trusting, and loving poetry enough while knowing and using the currencies of cultural and social fashion very well indeed. In the title of Bishop's "Sandpiper," for instance, readers of the third category (like those of the first and probably the second) miss Blake's "World in a Grain of Sand" from the *Auguries of Innocence* and his "piping down the valleys wild/Piping songs of pleasant glee" from the "Introduction" to the *Songs of Innocence*. They decide Bishop's poem is nothing other than a deconstruction of noumenal reality rather than reading the poem, as it may be read, as a gentle, generous resolution of natural and noumenal fact.

For readers of all three categories, poets such as Spenser and Milton, Blake and Hopkins, Emily Dickinson and Bishop, Rilke and Celan, Hector de Saint-Denys-Garneau and John Thompson – or (for all the differences among them) Jay Macpherson and Margaret Avison, Richard Outram and Robert Bringhurst – must remain either largely incomprehensible or confused. Think, for example, of Paul de Man's exasperated essay on one of Rilke's *Duino Elegies*. Sandpipers, on the other hand, seem to have no problem inhabiting all the metaphorical implications of both poetry and prose. That things as they are in words are other than nominal, that poetry too might be a natural thing, that a certain lamination of time, place, object, and word might also be lifted into a penultimate light are matters that seem immaterial to too many of us. Meister Eckhart wrote, "anyone who rests content merely with the sign will never get to the interior truth."[5]

For his part, Lyell, a dealer in rock hard facts, had no doubt that his methods as a geological thinker looking for truth were centrally dependent upon metaphorical, analogous reasoning. So convinced was he of the validity of analogically-arrived-at evidence that *The Principles of Geology* is subtitled with deliberately polemical provocation: *An Attempt to Explain the Former Changes of the Earth's Surface by Reference to Causes now in Operation.* Wherever he travelled, Lyell's analogical eye searched the springs, streams, rivers, currents, tides, landslips, and sedimentations of Nova Scotian landscape and seascape watchful to find, in the relatively small geophysical forces of the present, evidence analogous to the operations of those greater forces, prolonged over immense spans of anterior time, which shaped an apparently permanent earth of mountains, valleys, plains and estuaries, which buried forests and plants and transmuted them into coal, which interred deposits of shell and coral thousands of fathoms above and below the present sea level and made them mineral. After Lyell published his *Principles* it became possible to know earth as an entity as reflexive as language and language as a conveyance adequate to that reflexure.

72

Lyell read the earth like a poet who must feel the edges of words and the pattern of lock and release they set up within the groundmass of syntax. His scientific thinking was literally literate. For him, earth was a text. In a letter describing a day spent examining fossils on the cliffs at Joggins, overlooking Cumberland Basin on the Bay of Fundy, Lyell could write, without giving any sense of metaphorical overreach: "I never enjoyed the reading of a marvellous chapter of the big volume more."[6]

There is space here for only one detached example of Lyell's manner and mass of observation, thinking, and writing. It occurs in a passage in his *Elements of Geology*, originally published in 1838, which begins an explanation of the formation of large, pure, laminated beds of mineral deposit. "If we take a handful of quartzose sand, mixed with mica, and throw it into a clear running stream, we see the materials immediately sorted by the moving water, the grains of quartz falling almost directly to the bottom, while the plates of mica take a much longer time to sink through the water, and are carried farther down the stream. At the first instant the water is turbid, but almost immediately the flat surfaces of the plates of mica are seen all alone, reflecting a silvery light as they descend slowly to form a distinct micaceous lamina. The mica is the heavier mineral of the two, but it remains a longer time suspended in the fluid, owing to its greater extent of surface. It is easy, therefore, to perceive that where such mud is acted upon by a river or tidal current, the thin plates of mica will be carried farther, and not deposited in the same places as the grains of quartz; and since the force and velocity of the stream varies from time to time, layers of mica or of sand will be thrown down successively on the same area."[7] If that passage reminds us at times of the parable of the seed and the sower in Matthew 13:18–23, it tells us something about the nature of true parables and about the nature of nature as a field of complex, co-inherent forces. Nature, when described accurately, according to its modes of operation, is invariably emblematic. The question is not whether a poetry of nature can or cannot still be written validly, the question is whether poetry itself is nature. That, at least, is my intelligence of it.

The freshness, energy, inclusiveness, and coherence of Lyell's work and of his intellectual generosity secured him followers and friends. The greatest of them was younger than he by twelve years. Charles Darwin sailed from Devonport, England, on *H.M.S. Beagle* in December, 1831, one year after the publication of the first volume of Lyell's *The Principles of Geology.* The volume must have been among the books Darwin took with him. Whether he was able to secure the next two volumes which appeared during the course of the *Beagle's* five-year voyage I do not know. But four years into the voyage, in July, 1835, Darwin wrote from Lima, Peru, to his cousin and close friend, William Darwin Fox: "I am become a zealous disciple of Mr. Lyell's views, as known in his admirable book.

Geologizing in South America, I am tempted to carry parts to a greater extent even than he does."[8] Darwin was to dedicate the second edition of his *Journal of Researches* (1845) to Lyell "with grateful pleasure, as an acknowledgement that the chief part of whatever scientific merit this journal and the other works of the author may possess has been derived from studying the well-known and admirable *Principles of Geology*." In a letter to Lyell accompanying the gift of this edition, Darwin added, "Those authors ... who like you educate people's minds as well as teach them special facts, can never, I should think, have full justice done them except by posterity, for the mind thus insensibly improved can hardly perceive its own upward ascent."[9]

To read Darwin's *Journal* from the perspective of Lyell's methodology of analogy is to be reminded of an aside in Darwin's autobiographical notes, "in my excursions during the voyage of the *Beagle*, when I could take only a single volume, I always chose Milton."[10] Observations in the *Journal*, particularly those made on the Galapagos Archipelago are vivid with analogical possibilities. Perhaps that is one of the reasons why the *Journal* was one of Elizabeth Bishop's favourite books. In a letter dated July 8, 1971, she wrote, "Darwin is my favourite hero, almost."[11] Her affection for the *Journal* suggests the source for the

fifty-two

miserable small volcanoes I could climb

with a few slithery strides –
volcanoes dead as ash heaps

in Bishop's poem "Crusoe in England."[12] For when Darwin
landed on the beach of Chatham Island, the first island of the
Galapagos Archipelago he visited, he counted sixty "black
truncated cones" of miniature extinct volcanoes. Darwin's
account continues: "The entire surface of this part of the island
seems to have been permeated, like a sieve, by the subterra-
nean vapours: here and there the lava, whilst soft, has been
blown into great bubbles; and in other parts, the tops of cav-
erns similarly formed have fallen in, leaving circular pits with
steep sides. From the regular form of the many craters, they
gave to the country an artificial appearance, which vividly
reminded me of those parts of Staffordshire, where the great
iron-foundries are most numerous."[13]

   If Darwin's account of the volcanoes seems to free us into
a wider sense of possibility when compared to the words of
Bishop's Crusoe which I just quoted, it is not merely because
Darwin's account is longer. Two or three lines of poetry, if
they really are poetry, contain the gist of many more lines
of prose, and usually something more than prose can ever
manage. No. It is because Darwin's account, if we examine it
carefully, reveals itself, among other things, as a more com-
pressed, rapid, and complex run of overt simile and covert
metaphor. Bishop's Crusoe says only that the volcanoes are

as "dead as ash heaps." Darwin's words play around volcanic deadness with generative activity. Metaphorically considered, volcanic process in Darwin's account has turned the ground into a "sieve." (Runnels of water were strained through earth's mesh like the juice of stewed apricots.) Darwin's lava has been "blown into great bubbles." (A lens of soapy water escapes the circular catchment of thumb and forefinger and is shaped into an iridescent globe.) The circular pits of antique eruption give the earth "an artificial appearance." (A throw of clay on the wheel is spun, pulled and drawn into centrifugal concavity.) And Darwin is reminded of Staffordshire, the home (although he does not tell us this) of his maternal Wedgwood ancestors. (Ash piles, yes, but also slag piles, coke piles, a mucky black marl of cinders and coal dust, the scoriated upper laminations of nineteenth century industrialized desecration, and the air suffocatingly dense with the heat of a hundred or more furnaces and forges.)

Both Bishop's Crusoe and Darwin have their eyes fixed on an object. The object for Darwin is Chatham Island beach. But the object for Bishop's Crusoe is really himself. Bishop's Crusoe is, in effect, that frequent figure in twentieth century literature, the poet who is no longer a poet, the poet who cannot remember how to find analogies which will extend and define conditions beyond his or her own immediate existence and has settled instead for a level of analogy so restricted that it is little more than a production of selfhood at its most selfish. For this reason a few lines further into "Crusoe in England," Bishop has her Crusoe trying unsuccessfully to complete some lines from one of the most famous poems of analogy in English. All that Crusoe can remember is "The flash upon that inward eye,/which is the bliss ..." Darwin, who "took much delight in Wordsworth's and Coleridge's poetry" while he was preparing the *Journal* for publication, could easily have added the missing two words and supplied a title. Daffodils "flash upon that inward eye,/which is the bliss of solitude" in Wordsworth's "I Wandered Lonely as a Cloud."[14] No wonder Bishop's Crusoe is forgetful or has chosen to forget what is too self-accusatory to remember. Solitude for him is no bliss; it is the unbearable heaviness of a being in which he must endure the company of himself wherever he looks, whatever he sees, all fifty-two weeks of every burned-out year. His solipsism appropriates even depleted volcanoes, or to speak more accurately, his solipsism specializes in appropriating depleted volcanoes. Darwin, by contrast, re-situates their fragmentary truncation in the fabric of their manner of creation and their present groundmass. Darwin's description of Chatham Island beach is an egress from ego. Bishop's Crusoe is marooned on ego's island and his language expresses that condition accordingly. Whose account are we to believe? Bishop knew. She wrote "Crusoe in England" in the late 1960s. Two years later, undeterred by her Crusoe's narrative, she visited the Galapagos Archipelago, in August, 1971, and was to describe with delight seeing a vermilion flycatcher ("It is very tiny, bright red & black, really ruby-like") on Charles Island and "a pair of sea lions mating on James [Island] ... an excited bevy of young-lady seals surrounded them helpfully."[15]

But leave the lamination of Lyell, Darwin, Elizabeth Bishop, Bishop's Crusoe, volcanoes, sea lions, seals and vermilion flycatcher for a moment so that Lyell can travel from Wolfville, Kings County, Nova Scotia, in July, 1842 and re-enter this essay at another linked place. For Darwin was not the only young disciple, friend, and dedicator in Lyell's life. Lyell was about to meet a second, still little more than a student, who eventually became one of the most distinguished Canadian geologists of the nineteenth century. With him as guide and collaborator, Lyell made a geological excursion in August, 1842, immediately after the sandy pipe triumph, an excursion which gave a name and history to the silvery-white, translucent, vitreous, laminated rock I found in a galvanized-metal shed in South Maitland in 1988. He was John William Dawson, born in Pictou, Pictou County, Nova Scotia, in October, 1820, twenty-three years younger than Lyell, eleven years younger than Darwin.

Dawson was the child of Scottish immigrants who had come to Pictou early in the nineteenth century. He attended Pictou Academy where his boyhood's pleasure with natural history, especially with fossils and rocks, was encouraged and guided by that virtuoso of the Scottish Renaissance, Pictou Acade-

79

my's founder and Principal, the Reverend Thomas McCulloch, teacher, theologian, controversialist, novelist, and scientist, whose ornithological researches and collections were famous enough to induce John James Audubon, while returning from his voyage to Labrador and Newfoundland, to visit McCulloch in Pictou in August, 1833. Dawson's merchant father had lost most of his savings during the general commercial collapse in Nova Scotia throughout the mid-1820s. Therefore there was only enough money to send Dawson to study at Edinburgh University for one year, between 1840–1841, during which he was able to take an introductory course in geology. Like most of the greatest scientists of the nineteenth century (and all the great poets of any century), like both Lyell and Darwin, Dawson was for the most part self-trained. As part of his training he assembled a large collection of rocks and fossils and in doing so made himself known to coal-mine managers in the Pictou area, many of whom were employed by investors in England. To one of those managers Lyell bore a letter of introduction from England in July, 1842, and the manager, Alexander Ross, in turn introduced Lyell to Dawson.

Dawson knew Lyell's work before they met. *The Principles of Geology* had reached its sixth edition by 1840. It had become and was to remain one of the most important books in Dawson's intellectual life. We can obtain some sense of what meeting and working with Lyell meant to Dawson from a passage in a speech he delivered over thirty years later. He emphasized "the fresh and vivid interest, almost childlike, which every new truth awakened" in Lyell. He added, "This feeling is more or less that of every true naturalist. It depends on the clear perception of what is presented to us, and on the keen realisation of its relation to things previously known, and perhaps still more on the sudden breaking of those new relations upon the mind, as if with a flash of divine light."[16] Twenty years earlier, in 1855, Dawson had dedicated the first edition of his masterpiece (one of the masterpieces of expository analysis in Canadian literature), *Acadian Geology: An Account of the Geological Structure and Mineral Resources of Nova Scotia*, to Lyell, speaking of his "grateful sense of your kindness," of his "sincere gratitude and respect."

Appreciating the felt weight of such expressions may take more gratitude than we now possess in a century when intellectual gratitude is often part of commodity trading. Rather than repeat more words from Dawson's dedication and risk their dismissal, I will remember an instance of his collaboration with Lyell. Lyell had noticed, without immediately being able to explain it, that the interior of fossil trees in the Joggins deposits were commonly pillars of pure sandstone, although they intersected and were surrounded by alternating tipped or horizontal laminations of shale and sandstone. Dawson's analogical solution was to show Lyell forested swamps full of canoe birch (*Butula papylacea*) "looking externally sound and fresh, although consisting simply of a hollow cylinder with all the wood decayed and gone." Dawson had already concluded from the evidence of the canoe birch that the cores of the fossil trees had similarly rotted out before the bark, and that these empty cores had filled with light sediments as the trees were gradually submerged by sedimentary overlays and subsidence, during which one forest grew on top of its predecessor in a succession of strata which Dawson later calculated to be, at Joggins, more than three miles in depth.[17]

But now it is August, 1842. Lyell has spent "a week of intense heat" in Pictou, watching humming birds in the garden of Mr. Poole, the superintendent of the Albion Mines. The humming birds "remained for many seconds poised in the air, while sucking the flowers of several climbers trailed to the wall on the outside of the window, and in this position the head and body appeared motionless, brilliant with green and gold plumage, the wings invisible, owing to the rapidity of their motion. The sound was somewhat like that of our humming hawk-moths or sphinges, but louder. When they darted away they seemed to emit a flash of bright colour."[18] They were a further instance of new relations breaking upon his mind. Then, perhaps reluctantly because of the heat, Lyell and Dawson travelled by post-road stagecoach over the Cobequid divide separating the drainage system of the Gulf of St. Lawrence to the north from that of the Bay of Fundy to the south. They left the coach in Truro, Colchester County, at the head of Cobequid Bay, the eastern upper inlet of the Bay of Fundy. From there they travelled, perhaps on horseback, perhaps by carriage, ten miles to the southwest along the southern Fundy shore to a point where the Shubenacadie River meets the Bay. There, to quote Lyell, "we started at an early hour each morning in a boat, after the great tidal wave or bore had swept up the estuary, and were then carried ten, fifteen, or twenty miles with great rapidity up the river, after which as the tide ebbed, we came down at our leisure, landing quietly wherever we pleased, at various points where the perpendicular cliffs offered sections on the right or left bank."[19] Dawson's account of the tidal bore is more dramatic, "the torrent of red water enters all the channels, creeks, and estuaries; surging, whirling and foaming ... as the stranger sees the water gaining with noiseless and steady rapidity on the steep sides of banks and cliffs, a sense of insecurity creeps over him, as if no limit could be set to the advancing deluge. In a little time, however, he sees that the fiat, 'hitherto shalt thou come and no farther' has been issued to the great bay tide: its retreat commences, and the waters rush back as rapidly as they entered."[20] Bishop also witnessed the tidal bore, either on the Great Village River which is on the north shore of the Bay of Fundy, almost directly opposite the outflow of the Shubenacadie, or (as I suspect, without enough evidence to be sure) on the Salmon River at Truro. Her tidal bore, in the second stanza of "The Moose," plays not with Dawson's analogy of the biblical Flood, but with the protocol and procedure of Victorian house calls,

> where if the river
> enters or retreats
> in a wall of brown foam
> depends on if it meets
> the bay coming in,
> the bay not at home[21]

There should be a painting. It could be a variation upon "Kindred Spirits," painted by Asher Brown Durands in 1849, which depicts the poet William Cullen Bryant and the painter Thomas Cole, who was Durand's mentor, standing on a high ledge of rock overlooking a gorge in the Catskill Mountains. Through the gorge flows a small stream with civil truculence. The portrait of Lyell and Dawson might, in the manner of a Bartlett print, be entitled "Shooting the Shubenacadie Bore" and entertain generations with the insinuations of hilarious homonym. It would show Lyell and Dawson in a trim, clinker-built skiff scooting up river on the inflowing tide, backwards, bow turned to face the tidal race while they pulled their oars against the current to avoid broaching. Or the portrait might be entitled "A Geological Excursion on the Shubenacadie" and depict Lyell and Dawson disembarking on the salt-grassed shore of an inlet, each impeccably accoutered in hob-nailed boots, beeswaxed canvas leggings, fawn cavalry-twill breeches and full-skirted coats of oatmeal Scottish tweed, baggy with bellows pockets. Both men shoulder leather specimen satchels. Both carry geological hammers. Each wears a wide-awake hat. Lyell's is grey, Dawson's green. The inlet is also the outlet of a small, shallow stream named Dow Creek. At low tide, the inlet will be revealed as a triangular sluice of red mud with steeply sloping sides forty feet deep. Now, at high tide, it is one of the few places along the immediate stretch of river which Lyell and Dawson are examining where they need not stalk awkwardly on steadily-higher heel stilts of viscid mud and climb cliffs to reach the stepped plateaus carved by successive eocene seas which rise from the Shubenacadie's west bank and run in a tier of four into the back country. Dawson ties the skiff's bow painter to a canoe birch leaning out over the inlet. Then he and Lyell start to walk up the bed of the stream flowing into the inlet. Immediately they are in a deep, narrow ravine with walls formed of tilted plates of black laminated limestone and loose limestone marls. The stream's bed suddenly swerves south, deflected by an outcrop of limestone. Lyell and Dawson disappear behind the outcrop. They escape into art. Fiction becomes us.

Let them go. The inlet, the birch, the stream bed, the stream, the ravine, the outcrop of limestone are all part of the farm where my wife and I live. If Lyell and Dawson continue on their way up the ravine of Dow Creek, they will be doing what I am sure they must have done, although there is no record of it in what they wrote. There are too few similarly convenient landing places along the particular reach of the Shubenacadie in question for them not to have done so, and it was a reach which Lyell's *Travels in North America* and Dawson's *Acadian Geology* show they examined with great geological attention. Let them go. They continue, out of our sight, following the stream bed and ravine as they work westward, away from the river; and the walls of the ravine lower gradually until, after five hundred yards, the stream's bed becomes a rocky, shallow trench almost level with a hay field. Thousands of black, metallically glinting alderflies swarm into flight around them as Dawson and Lyell push through the brush growing along the stream. They stand clear in the hayfield and glance at the ground upon which the house where my wife and I live was to be built in 1915. In that same year, using in part evidence which Lyell and Dawson had accumulated, the German geophysicist, Alfred Wegener, restored the Platonic analogy of Atlantis from the nominal to the real by postulating Pangaea, the mid-Atlantic super-continent whose disintegration and drift account for the radical foldings, crumplings, and anticlinal tilts of strata about which Lyell and Dawson were so speculative and for which they could offer no full explanation.[22] I watch them both from an upstairs window. They talk briefly, then turn and begin to walk down the eastward slope of the hayfield toward the river's level. Like us, they do not feel the slight spring of earth as Nova Scotia continues its slow recoil from lifted glacial weight. When they reach the bottom of the field where it becomes filled with new growth birch and spruce, they find a path I cut late last spring with a chainsaw. Its way leads along the northern edge of Dow Creek ravine and back to the moored skiff.

If or as they rowed out of the inlet and looked north downriver, toward the Bay of Fundy, Lyell and Dawson could see the part of the Shubenacadie about which they both wrote the most. "On the west side," recorded Dawson, "is an immense mass of gypsum named White's or the Big Plaster Rock, and one of the principal localities of the extensive gypsum-trade of this river. The Big Rock at one time presented ... a snowy front of gypsum, nearly 100 feet in height ... it is a massive bed arranged in thick layers, and the whole bent into an arched or almost cylindrical form."[23] Of the same sequence of "gypsiferous strata," Lyell commented: "The general strike of the beds ... is nearly east and west, the strata seeming to have been first folded into numerous parallel wrinkles, running east and west, and then parts of these folds tilted at considerable angles, sometimes to the east, and sometimes to the west, while the rocks were fissured in the direction of their strike and shifted vertically ... At the Big Rock, a mass of gypsum or alabaster of a pure white colour and no less than 300 yards thick, is exposed and forms a conspicuous object in the vertical cliff, and has been followed continuously east and west for 12 miles through the country."[24]

Does syntax follow the flex of earth in such matters, or does earth follow a measure of syntax which language emulates? Knowing what art it takes to contrive the former, I am ready to believe the latter, as also to discover in Dawson's and Lyell's accounts of White's or the Big Rock a name or names for the silvery-white, vitreous, translucent slab I found among sawdust and shavings in a galvanized-metal shed in 1988. For Lyell's description of the Big Rock deposit continues, "Below it are alternations of anhydrous gypsum," and Dawson's, "In its lower part there is much anhydrite."

"Anhydrous gypsum" or "anhydrite," what does it look like? Gypsum I knew only as almost everyone knows it: a friable, chalky, amorphous substance. I knew it only as plaster, as a white filling sandwiched between the thin cardboard slices of a gyprock sheet, as a white powder mixed with water to make the paste with which to patch and prepare a wall for papering or for painting and as an almost endlessly infiltrative dust throughout the house after renovation and redecorating. But as a substance of more resistant structure I did not know it. Only by comparing Lyell's and Dawson's accounts of the lowermost laminations of the Big Rock deposit with a description Dawson made of another gypsum deposit in Nova Scotia on the St. Croix River, not far from Wolfville, did I find gypsum's other possible qualities. "This cliff," Dawson wrote, "consists principally of the variety of gypsum named ... 'sharkstone' by the quarrymen ... referring to the rough shagreen-like texture of its weathered surfaces. It is *Anhydrite* or gypsum destitute of the combined water, which gives to the ordinary variety its softness and usefulness as a material for modelling and plastering. Anhydrite may, however, be used as a substitute for marble."[25] A passage in Lyell's *Elements of Geology* laminates the matter further: "Anhydrous gypsum is a rare variety, into which water does not enter as a component part ... A variety of it, alabaster, is a granular and compact variety of gypsum found in masses large enough to be used in sculpture and architecture. It is sometimes a pure snow-white substance, as that of Volterra in Tuscany, well known as being carved for works of art in Florence and Leghorn. It is a softer stone than marble and more easily wrought."[26] So, to return to Pound, this time to "Hugh Selwyn Mauberley," when

> The "age demanded" chiefly a mould in plaster
> Made with no loss of time,
> A prose kinema, not assuredly alabaster
> Or the "sculpture" of rhyme[27]

what the age rejected (alabaster) was the same basic substance as what it demanded (gypsum). And the age has been doubly self-condemned by the stultification of its choice.

Is that what Pound meant; or are we dealing only with

an opportunity of rhyme? When words are mined for their origins in earth, we may find ourselves speaking in tongues, in structures of metaphor and analogy we cannot always control. To Lyell and Dawson, my silvery-white translucent rock would have been a specimen of anhydrite. To their quarrymen contemporaries on the St. Croix, it would have been "shark-stone"; and the "shagreen" to which their analogical designation referred was the "shark-skin rough with natural papillae used for rasping and polishing" which those of us in an economy of more synthetically contrived abrasives have never even seen.[28] As for Pound, I doubt whether he would have recognized in the rock much more than an insufficiently structured possibility. And modernity, what would it call the rock? First, "gypsum," from the Greek "*gypsos*" meaning plaster. Then, more specifically, "selenite," from the Greek "*selenites*" meaning "moonstone." In current geological taxonomy, selenite and alabaster are both classified together as the dense gypsums.[29] But I will give the rock a name myself, one which is and is not mine, and will remember that Jacob Boehme wrote (in John Sparrow's seventeenth-century translation), "For understand thy *Mother Tongue aright*, thou hast as deep a Ground *therein*, as there is in the *Hebrew*, or *Latine* ..." or, I add (to suit this case) "*Greeke.*" I find the name "spar" from the Anglo-Saxon "*spaer*" or "*spaeren,*" meaning "gypsum."[30]

If anyone parry by saying that, as a noun in common use now, "spar" can only evoke a vessel at sea, still let it stand. Even though anhydrous by nature, what else is spar but a vessel of sea compacted? To some people spar may be as common as water. To others it is immortal diamond. Before I was human, sea lay over the earth where I write. Shells and corals disintegrated in tides and currents. As lees they sank into tidal lagoons. They were titrated by cycles of flood and drought. They pressed against precessional layers of themselves and, in turn, were levelled into lamination by deposits above them. Spar is their compacted translucence holding still something of the sun that shone when it was finally composed. Spar is the original substance remaining of unique water. Upon its surface are the last flaws of wind and flow before they became mineral. Spar is the edge of its own word. When I was a child I was taught to read by having to find named letters made of wood which had been tossed into a bin in the centre of the classroom. As I brought each letter back to my teacher, I felt the edge of its shape with my fingers. I feel the edge of spar in my hand. Spar is the crystal I lift. Words may only be witness to light, but they do bear witness.

In the *Revelation* there is "a sea of glass like unto crystal" which supports the throne of God and the four evangelists of the word, Matthew, Mark, Luke, and John, who appear as theriomorphic beasts giving "glory and honour and thanks," those gifts of poetry as well as prayer. The sea of glass reappears in a later chapter of *Revelation* where those "having the harps of God" sing the "song of Moses." Let us say that spar is no sea of glass. Let us say only that spar is one of that sea's analogies and certain possibilities of speech become unproscribable. Therefore William Law wrote in the introductory dialogue he provided for the work of Boehme, "Everything that exists or thinks or moves or finds itself in any kind or Degree of Sensibility, is from, and out of this glassy Sea."[31] And Christina Rossetti in her commentary on *Revelation* wrote of the glassy sea's surface "reflecting all which surrounds it ... a figure of that which (God willing) will convey ... Everything which is very good, all things lovely, the height of the heaven in comparison of the earth, the wide distance of the east from the west, all will be seen and known."[32] Law and Rossetti are speaking of apocatastasis, renewal, rebirth, when the word and the world, when the sign and the signified celebrate their marriage in Jerusalem, the restored paradise which may be lost as much by a passive negligence of memory as by an active misapplication of will.

Perhaps, as Blake thought, we can assist at the hierogamy of word and middle earth if we have eyes to see. Perhaps apocatastasis, like spar, is immediately present. In the traditions of Chinese art, it is not always possible to tell if a rock is small or large. It might be the size of a large hand, held palm upward with fingers extended. It could be the uncarved block of stone which appears in some translations of *Tao Tê Ching*.[33] It could be the stone which the builders refused in Psalm 118. Or it could be the size of an island. I think again of Darwin's visit to

Charles Island in 1835 and am riddled by his description of "a small boy sitting by a well with a switch in his hand, with which he killed the doves and finches as they came to drink. He had already procured a little heap of them for his dinner; and he said that he had constantly been in the habit of waiting by this well for the same purpose. It would appear that the birds of this archipelago, not having as yet learnt that man is a more dangerous animal than the tortoise or Amblyrhynychus, disregard him, in the same manner as in England shy birds, such as magpies, disregard the cows and horses grazing in our fields."[34] I think also of Elizabeth Bishop's Crusoe, on the same island, who dyes

> a baby goat bright red
> with my red berries, just to see
> something a little different
> and then his mother wouldn't recognize him.[35]

Perhaps the conclusion to be drawn from both passages is that Eden is everywhere as is also eastward of Eden, and that we concede too easily that our arts can only be practised in what we choose to think of as the only way of the world. If no man is an island, so now no island is insular, not even the island of this earth whose image, stilling its spin in the analogical space of a photograph, intimates dependence upon a maker of images. "You can have no real knowledge of Nature and its inward working Power," wrote Law in his introduction to Boehme, "But so far as the Workings of Nature, and the Birth of Things, are Working and a Birth in yourself."[36]

Early one morning last spring I was walking down by the Shubenacadie. It was low tide. When I reached the outflow of Dow Creek I stopped, as usual, to scan the deposits of black, low, rounded limestone whose upper laminations strike just below the river bank. One smooth, low mound of limestone suddenly shifted and was transformed into two otters running and swimming along the moving tide line, always touching each other as if they could never be anything else but continuous, each with the other, in a dance of intricate pleasure, in a flux and flow which were a re-enactment of water and an incarnation of their element. I was able, for a little space, to follow them further until they finally resolved into the liminal groundmass of middle distance, leaving foot-prints here and there wherever their way had crossed traps of red mud and making a narration I could, for once, partly recount. For the full language of earth has not been deciphered. The signature of things is still being written. Our words have no meaning without its concordance.

Afterword

The Token

I took the ring and gave myself to earth.
Nothing attended. Nothing shaped the air.
What other reason could I have for love.

Beside the river wove a secret path.
Somehow I guessed its ending nebular.
I took the ring and gave myself to earth.

How can I say all things within you move?
To speak of near is knowing them as far.
What other reason could I have for love.

Below can break the mirror of above.
A hidden thrush acutes the sharpened air.
I took the ring and gave myself to earth.

Marrying moves the carriage of my breath.
Nothing proposed that everything was clear.
No other reason brought me to my love.

Looking for life I interceded death.
Given the ways I turned them circular.
I took the ring and gave myself to earth.
What other reason could I have for love.

Notes

EPIGRAPHS

The first epigraph is taken from Franz Pfeiffer, *Meister Eckhart*, trans. C. de B.Evans, vol. 1 of 2 (London: John M. Watkins, 1956) pg. 193.

The second epigraph comes from Eckhart's sermon, *"Justi vivent in aeternum,"* part of which is translated in Reiner Schürmann, *Meister Eckhart: Mystic and Philosopher* (Bloomington and London: Indiana University Press, 1978) pg. 104.

FOREWORD

1.   H.D. Thoreau, *Excursions* (Boston: Ticknor and Fields, 1863) pp. 161–162.
2.   W.W. Skeat, *An Etymological Dictionary of the English Language* (Oxford: Clarendon Press; and New York: Macmillan and Co., 1882) pg. 527.

BIORACHAN ROAD

The essay originally appeared in *The Fiddlehead*, Spring 1984, No. 139. Its main source of historical information is G. R. Sutherland, *The Rise and Decline of the Community of Earltown* (Truro, NS: Colchester Historical Museum, 1980).

The essay was first published in *The Antigonish Review*, Autumn 1987 – Winter 1988, No. 71–72.

1.   J. MacPhee, *The Survival of the Bark Canoe* (New York: Farrar, Straus, Giroux, 1975) pg. 14.

2.   E.T. Adney and H.I. Chappelle, *The Bark Canoes and Skin Boats of North America* (Washington, DC: Smithsonian Institution Press, 1983) pg. 23.

3.   E. Pound, *Selected Letters: 1907–1941* (New York: New Directions, 1971) pg. 248.

4.   J. Donne, *The Sermons of John Donne*, vol. 9 of 10 (Berkeley and Los Angeles: University of California Press, 1962) pg. 134.

5.   E. Neumann, *The Origins and History of Consciousness*, vol. 2 of 2 (New York: Harper & Brothers, 1962) pg. 276.

6.   Donne, loc. cit.

7.   Lao Tzu, *Tao Tê Ching*, trans. by D.C. Lau (Harmondsworth, Middlesex, England: Penguin Books Ltd., 1963) pg. 86.

8.   E. Carpenter, *Eskimo Realities* (New York: Holt, Rinehart and Winston, 1973) pg. 43.

KEEPING: THE CAMERON YARD

First publication of the essay was in *The Antigonish Review*, Winter 1991, No. 84.

1.   C. Eldridge, *Eldridge's Coast Pilot, No. 1, Eastern Section from Chatham to Canso, N.S., Including the Bay of Fundy* (Boston: S. Thaxter and Son, 1884) pg. 317.

2.   N. Bowditch, *The American Practical Navigator* ... (New York: E. & G. W. Blunt, 1844) pg. 314.

3.   F. W. Wallace, *Wooden Ships and Iron Men* (London: Hodder and Stoughton, 1924) pp. 145, 161, 304–305, 315, 318.

4.   J. Ortega y Gassett, *The Dehumanization of Art* (Garden City, New York: Doubleday, Anchor Books, N.D.) pg. 77.

5.   W. H. Auden, *The Dyer's Hand and Other Essays* (London: Faber and Faber, 1963) pp. 51–52.

6.   C. S. Singleton, *Dante Alighieri, The Divine Comedy, Paradiso, 2, Commentary*, Bollingen Series LXXX, (Princeton, NJ: Princeton University Press, 1975) pg. 309.

7.   J. Ciardi, *The Divine Comedy, Dante Alighieri* (New York: W. W. Norton & Company Ltd., 1977) pg. 506.

8.   J. Donne, *Donne's Sermons: Selected Passages, with an Essay by Logan Pearsall Smith* (Oxford: Clarendon Press, 1964) pg. 142. Donne uses the psalm number of the *Book of Common Prayer* and the King James Version. The Vulgate number is Psalm 18 (*Caeli enarrant*).

9.   Ciardi, op. cit., pg. 509.

GROUNDMASS

This is the essay's first appearance.

1.   Ezra Pound, *Drafts & Fragments of Cantos* CX–CXVII (New York: New Directions, 1968) pg. 25.

2.   S. T. Coleridge, *Anima Poetae*, ed. E. H. Coleridge (London: William Heinemann, 1895) pg. 173.

3.   Charles Lyell, *Travels in North America*, vol. 2 of 2 (New York: Wiley and Putnam, 1845) pp. 141–42. The slab of mud and sandpiper tracks are illustrated, full size, in a lithograph facing pg. 142.

4.   Bishop's poem is briefly discussed in the editorial, *Elizabeth Bishop Society of Nova Scotia Newsletter* (Spring 2001, vol. 8.1). The discussion includes a quotation from Frye's *Fearful Symmetry*: "No student of Blake can fail to be deeply impressed by the promptness with

which Blake seizes on the machine as the symbol of a new kind of human existence developing in his own time."

5. Franz Pfeiffer, *Meister Eckhart*, trans. C. de B. Evans, vol. 1 of 2 (London: John M. Watkins, 1956) pg. 193.

6. Charles Lyell, *Life, Letters and Journals*, vol. 2 of 2 (London: John Murray, 1881) pg. 181.

7. Charles Lyell, *The Student's Elements of Geology* (London: John Murray, 1878) pg. 16.

8. Charles Darwin, *The Life and Letters*, ed. F. Darwin, vol. 1 of 3 (London: John Murray, 1888) pg. 263.

9. Ibid, pp. 337–338.

10. Ibid, pg. 69.

11. Elizabeth Bishop, *One Art: Letters*, ed. R. Giroux (New York: Farrar, Straus, Giroux, 1994) pg. 544.

12. Elizabeth Bishop, *The Complete Poems: 1927–1979* (New York: Farrar, Straus, Giroux, 1983) pp. 162–166.

13. Charles Darwin, *Journal of Researches* (London: John Murray, 1890) pg. 359.

14. Charles Darwin, *The Life and Letters*, vol. 1, pg. 69.

15. Elizabeth Bishop, *One Art*, pg. 591. Bishop's letter to Frani Blough Muser is dated December 14, 1974.

16. William Dawson, *Fifty Years of Work in Canada, Scientific and Educational* (London: Ballantyne, Hanson & Co., 1900) pg. 54.

17. Charles Lyell, *The Student's Elements of Geology*, pp. 401–403.

18. Charles Lyell, *Travels in North America*, vol. 2, pp. 191–192.

19. Ibid, pg. 192.

20. William Dawson, *Acadian Geology* (Edinburgh: Oliver and Boyd, 1855) pg. 24.

21. Elizabeth Bishop, *The Complete Poems*, pg. 169.

22. Alfred Lothar Wegener (1880–1930) published *Die Entstehung der Kontinente und Ozeane* in 1915. The consequence of his book is developed in the main, modern authority on Nova Scotian geology, Albert E. Roland's *Geological Background and Physiography of Nova Scotia* (Halifax: The Nova Scotian Institute of Science, for the Nova Scotia Museum, 1982).

23. William Dawson, *Acadian Geology*, pp. 231–232.

24. Charles Lyell, *Travels in North America*, vol. 2, pg. 179.

25. William Dawson, *Acadian Geology*, pg. 225.

26. Charles Lyell, *The Student's Elements of Geology*, pp. 14–15.

27. Ezra Pound, *Personae: The Collected Shorter Poems* (New York: New Directions, 1971) pg. 188.

28. *The Concise Oxford English Dictionary*, entry for "shagreen."

29. Charles W. Chesterman, *The Audubon Society Field Guide to North American Rocks and Minerals* (New York: Alfred A. Knopf, 1978) pp. 459–460.

30. Jacob Boehme, *Aurora*, trans. J. Sparrow (London: John Streater for Giles Calvert, 1656) pg. 146.

31. William Law, *The Way to Divine Knowledge* (1752), in *Law's Works*, ed. B. Moreton, vol. 7 (reprinted by Georg Olms Verlag, Hildesheim, New York, 1974), pg. 213.

32. Christina Rossetti, *The Face of the Deep: A Devotional Commentary on the Apocalypse* (London: Society for Promoting Christian Knowledge, 1895) pg. 156. Rossetti's book is the most neglected of the essays of consequence on poetics in English.

33. See, for example, Arthur Waley, *The Way and Its Power: A Study of the Tao Tê Ching and Its Place in Chinese Thought* (New York: Grove Weidenfield, 1958) pg. 211. The uncarved block appears in Chapter VLII of the *Tao Tê Ching*. Its counterpart in Chang Chung-yun's *Tao: A New Way of Thinking* (New York: Harper & Row, 1975), pg. 157, is, apparently, "original simplicity." A distrust of analogy similar to Ciardi's might be involved.

34. Charles Darwin, *Journal of Researches*, pg. 383.

35. Elizabeth Bishop, *The Complete Poems*, pg. 165.

36. William Law, op. cit., pg. 202.

Acknowledgements

Peter Thomas began this book by commissioning "Biorachan Road" for *The Fiddlehead*. As editors of *The Antigonish Review*, George and Gertrude Sanderson made a place for "The Crooked Knife" and "Keeping: The Cameron Yard." Andrew Steeves, in turn, brought all three essays down from their attic of indexes. I am very grateful to him. Collaboration with the photographer Thaddeus Holownia on *The Third Hand* and *Ironworks* managed part of the way in "Keeping: The Cameron Yard." Steven Skipper lent me geology in a long conversation. I also thank Marie Law for her patience with archaeological overlays and Joanne Campbell for finding the names. As copy editors, Clare Goulet and Kathleen Martin saw and heard. Wesley Bates found the grain of light in the grain of stone. My friend, the late Edgar Murphy of Balmoral, Colchester County, taught me how to hang an axe, and he made sure I never ran out of wood. The dedication is to my wife and her slow unfoldings of silk.

Amethyst is a typeface designed
in four weights by Jim Rimmer at the
Rimmer Type Foundry, New Westminster, BC.
This is its first showing in book form.

The images reproduced throughout were
engraved on maple blocks by Wesley Bates.
They are reproduced at their original size.

Typeset in Amethyst by Andrew Steeves and printed offset at
Gaspereau Press by Gary Dunfield and Marilyn MacIntyre.

Gaspereau Press acknowledges the support of the Canada Council
for the Arts and the Nova Scotia Department of Tourism and Culture.

1   3   5   4   2

NATIONAL LIBRARY OF CANADA CATALOGUING IN PUBLICATION

Sanger, Peter, 1943–
Spar : words in place / Peter Sanger.

ISBN 1-894031-55-5 (BOUND)
ISBN 1-894031-54-7 (PAPER)

1. Title.
PS 8587.A372S63 2002   c814'.54   c2002–901428–x
PR9199.3.S22S63 2002

GASPEREAU PRESS, PRINTERS & PUBLISHERS
ONE CHURCH AVENUE, KENTVILLE, NOVA SCOTIA
CANADA B4N 1K7